# Fishing

Written by Ann Love with Jane Drake
Illustrated by Pat Cupples

Kids Can Press

"Oh, he's a keeper!" Grandma says. She reaches to hold Jessie's new baby brother before they're even through the door.

"What's a 'keeper'?" asks Jessie.

"An oldtimer's word for a fish worth keeping," Grandpa laughs.

Jessie sits on the front step and looks down the Maine coastline. She and her mother have traveled all the way from southeastern Alaska to visit Grandma and Grandpa and to show off her brother. She's tired and misses Dad, who couldn't come on this trip.

"I'm going to check my fish farm now," says Grandpa. "Want to come? You can choose a fish for supper."

"Sure," Jessie says. "Let's go."

2

They putt away from the wharf in Grandpa's dory. Grandpa points to a large fishing boat out in the bay.

"That's a trawler. It carries a net that opens so wide underwater it could catch an ice rink full of fish," Grandpa shouts above the noise of the engine.

The huge net is towed behind the trawler on long cables. For years, trawl nets dragged the sea bottom, where groundfish live, and hauled up tons of cod, halibut and flounder. Too many were caught, so today groundfish are in shorter supply. A few trawlers still fish near the coast, but most have to travel far out to sea.

trawler

4

dory

trawl net

"See that longliner?" Grandpa points to a boat on shore. "It's not used anymore."

Longliners catch groundfish near wrecks and rocks, where a trawl net might snag. While the longliner chugs forward, the crew shoots a hooked and baited groundline off the back of the boat. When the line settles on the ocean floor, groundfish bite the bait and get hooked.

With fewer groundfish left to catch, many longliners now lie abandoned, and their crews are out of work.

"Grandpa, if there aren't lots of groundfish left, what can we take home for supper?" asks Jessie.

"A tasty farmed fish," Grandpa answers.

groundline

longliner

7

"Some of us in the village have learned to farm fish—mostly Atlantic salmon," Grandpa explains. "I'm trying to farm halibut too. People love the way halibut tastes, but there aren't many wild ones to catch anymore."

Fish farmers grow salmon in floating net pens that are anchored to the ocean bottom in sheltered coves. Grandpa's farm has twelve pens strapped together and connected with walkways. Some net pens hold small fish, others larger fish, and at least one pen holds fish big enough to sell.

Every day, workers ride their dories out to the net pens to feed the fish. When a buyer places an order, workers catch the fish with a hand net, kill and clean them, then pack them in insulated boxes for shipping.

"But how do you get the fish to live in these pens?" Jessie asks. "And can't the little ones just swim out the holes?"

"Let's go to the hatchery and you'll see," says Grandpa.

"Fish farming begins here in a hatchery. Workers collect eggs from captive adult fish," Grandpa explains. "The eggs hatch on screens in these water-filled trays. Take a peek at the newly hatched salmon fry."

"Oh! They're see-through and small, like mosquitoes," Jessie says.

The salmon fry are soon moved into freshwater tanks where they grow quickly. When they are the length of Grandpa's hand, they are called smolts and are big enough to move into net pens in the sea. There the smolts are fed food pellets several times a day until they are full grown, about 18 months later.

"Here's where we grow halibut," says Grandpa. "Freshly hatched halibut are so small, we can keep hundreds in one pail. The ones in these tanks are more than five months old."

"Halibut sure look weird," remarks Jessie. "Every one of them has both eyes on the same side of its head!"

A halibut hatches with one eye on each side of its head, but by the time the fish is five months old the left eye has traveled over the top of the head and settled on the right side. Then the halibut can lie hidden in the sand, waiting for smaller fish to swim by so it can eat them.

"We don't know yet whether it's best to grow the adults in net pens or in huge in-ground tanks. Halibut farming is still experimental," Grandpa explains.

"Wow, the halibut in this tank are as big as you, Grandpa," Jessie says.

"Yes," agrees Grandpa. "We get our eggs from these fish."

To make it easy for workers to collect eggs from such huge fish, scientists have invented an underwater cot. Workers herd the halibut onto the cot and raise it to the surface of the tank, where they quickly gather the eggs.

As fish farmers and scientists try raising different kinds of fish, such as salmon and halibut, rules have to be made so that the fish farms don't pollute the sea and harm wild fish.

"Farming keeps our fishing way of life alive until there are lots of wild fish to catch again," says Grandpa.

"Let's go find some farmed salmon to eat," Jessie suggests.

"And make fish cakes," Grandpa says. "They're my favorite."

halibut

14

halibut cot

15

"Have you ever seen a halibut cot?" Jessie asks Dad when she arrives home in Alaska.

"Never," he replies. "We do have fish hatcheries up here, but in many places there are still wild fish to catch."

"Are you sure people aren't catching too many?" asks Jessie.

"You've been talking to your grandpa," Dad says, "and it's a good point. My job is to stop overfishing of Pacific salmon and help all wild fish whenever I can."

"You have the best job," Jessie tells Dad. "Can I go to work with you?"

"OK," says Dad, "but get packing. Salmon cover a lot of territory. Fish and wildlife officers like me have to keep track of all the different kinds. We travel hundreds of miles just to keep up with the salmon."

Pacific salmon mate and lay their eggs on the gravelly bottom of the same clear stream in which they were born. Then the adults die. After the eggs hatch, the young salmon grow in the shaded stream or a nearby lake for one or two years.

Fish and wildlife officers work closely with state biologists to keep an eye on salmon streams. Because salmon lay their eggs in loose gravel, officers and biologists make sure no one removes gravel from the stream beds or packs it down with heavy equipment. In some areas, fisheries workers even help the fish by raking away leaves and carefully adding fresh, loose gravel. Officers and biologists also check that no trees growing beside the streams are cut down. Trees shade the streams, and tree roots hold the soil so it doesn't fall in and muddy the water. Newly hatched salmon stay healthier in clear streams.

After one or two summers, the young salmon leave their birth streams and swim down rivers to the sea. They spend several years feasting on fish and shrimp in the Pacific Ocean. Then the adults swim back upriver, jumping rapids and small waterfalls. Each salmon knows exactly where it was born and returns to that spot, the females to lay their eggs, and the males to fertilize them.

"No one knows how the salmon find their way," Dad says.

If people dam a salmon river, the state may construct a fishway around the dam as a detour for the fish. Sometimes fishways are built beside waterfalls to make the hard journey upriver easier. At the top of a fishway, fish counters record how many salmon travel each way.

"One of the toughest parts of my job, Jessie, is patrolling river mouths where salmon rivers meet the ocean," Dad says. "That's where people like to build towns, pulpmills and factories. And that could mean lots of pollution to poison the salmon. Limits are set and I check that they're obeyed."

In summer, adult salmon return to the river mouths to start their hard trip upriver to mate. Ocean-going fishing boats move in for the catch.

The State Board of Fisheries decides how many salmon can be harvested and the size of the nets that can be used. State biologists mark off "no fishing" areas so enough salmon get past the nets and upriver to mate. At any time, the state can make the safe areas bigger so there will be salmon to fish in years to come.

"There's a big seiner fishing for salmon," says Dad.

"How did the crew know the salmon were there?" Jessie asks.

"They waited and watched for salmon jumping out of the water," answers Dad. "Then they set out a big, deep net that surrounded the fish. Now the crew is bringing in the net full of fish."

Fish and wildlife officers in patrol boats may ask the seiners to call in the number and kind of salmon they have caught that day. Sometimes officers board fishing boats to inspect the catch and equipment to be sure all the rules are followed. Everyone needs to work together to make sure the salmon aren't overfished.

seiner

A boat called a gillnetter is also used to catch returning salmon. The gillnetter lets down a fencelike net across the path of the fish. One end of the net is usually attached to the back of the boat and the other end to a big float called a buoy. The net drifts with the boat, and all big fish swimming into it are caught by their own gills. When the crew thinks the net is full, a motor helps them pull it in by wrapping the net around a drum.

A tender boat stands nearby, ready to take the fish to a processing plant. There they are killed, gutted, weighed, canned or frozen and shipped to market. The heads and guts are chopped up and turned into fertilizer.

gillnetter

gillnet

buoy

On the way home, Jessie and Dad stop at a fishwheel operated by the state. Here, biologists catch salmon partway upriver. The fish are alive in the wheel, so workers can safely study the salmon and then let them go.

"Let's stop and buy a salmon to take home for dinner, Dad," says Jessie. "We'll choose one big enough that Grandpa would call it a keeper."

After supper, Jessie phones Grandpa.
"Hi there," she says. "We've got some great wild salmon out
here, and we need your yummy fish cakes recipe for the leftovers."

# Jessie's and Grandpa's Fish Cakes

*Serves 2–3*

**You'll need:**

1 cup (250 mL) cooked, flaked salmon,
   flounder (sole) or halibut

1 egg, beaten in a bowl

2 cups (500 mL) mashed potatoes

¼ teaspoon (1 mL) salt

2 tablespoons (30 mL) milk

1 tablespoon (15 mL) chopped parsley

2 tablespoons (30 mL) butter or
   ¼ cup (60 mL) vegetable oil

1 cup (250 mL) breadcrumbs

a frying pan and flipper or spatula

an adult to help with the frying

**1.** Mix the fish, beaten egg, mashed potatoes,
salt, milk and parsley in a bowl.

**2.** Shape the mixture into balls in your hand
and then flatten them into patties.

**3.** Add the butter or oil to the frying pan and
heat until it bubbles.

**4.** Dip each patty in the breadcrumbs and
lay it in the hot frying pan.

**5.** Cook on each side 2 or 3 minutes or
until the patty turns golden brown.

Serve hot.

# Index

Dedicated to memories of Captain Small, Harry Yard, Willie White
and the Barnett family visits to the Maine Coast.

The authors gratefully acknowledge the assistance of Bob Clay,
Robert Cook, Gillian Lee, Matt Litvak, Joanne McCormick, Tom Moffatt,
Sue Leppington, Ike Lorenz, Ann Prendergast, Gene Rajadan, and Ken Waiwood.

Thanks to Valerie Hussey, Ricky Englander and all the people at Kids Can Press.
Thanks to Pat Cupples, whose imaginative illustrations bring life to even the
most technical of details. A special thank you to Laura Ellis, Elizabeth MacLeod, Trudee Romanek and
Debbie Rogosin, whose editorial touches added warmth to chilled waters.

First U.S. edition 1999

Text copyright © 1997 by Ann Love and Jane Drake
Illustrations copyright © 1997 by Pat Cupples

The artwork in this book was rendered in watercolor, gouache,
graphite and colored pencil on hot-press watercolor paper.

All rights reserved. No part of this publication may be reproduced,
stored in a retrieval system or transmitted, in any form or by any
means, without the prior written permission of Kids Can Press Ltd.
or, in case of photocopying or other reprographic copying, a
license from CANCOPY (Canadian Copyright Licensing Agency),
1 Yonge Street, Suite 1900, Toronto, ON, M5E 1E5.

Published in Canada by          Published in the U.S. by
Kids Can Press Ltd.             Kids Can Press Ltd.
29 Birch Avenue                 85 River Rock Drive, Suite 202
Toronto, ON  M4V 1E2            Buffalo, NY 14207

Edited by Debbie Rogosin and Trudee Romanek
Designed by Marie Bartholomew and Karen Powers
Printed in Hong Kong by Sheck Wah Tong Printing Press Limited.

US 99 0 9 8 7 6 5 4 3 2 1

**Canadian Cataloguing in Publication Data**

Love, Ann
        Fishing
(America at work)
Includes index.

ISBN 1-55074-457-7

1. Fisheries – United States – Juvenile literature. I. Drake, Jane. II.
Cupples, Patricia. III. Title. IV. Series: America at work
(Toronto,Ont)

SH223.L68      1999a      j639.2'0973      C99-930802-5

Kids Can Press is a Nelvana company